KENT IN PHOTOGRAPHS

BRYAN PHILLIPS

AMBERLEY

First published 2019

Amberley Publishing
The Hill, Stroud
Gloucestershire, GL5 4EP

www.amberley-books.com

ISBN 978 1 4456 8666 0 (print)
ISBN 978 1 4456 8667 7 (ebook)

British Library Cataloguing in Publication Data.
A catalogue record for this book is available from the British Library.

Typesetting by Aura Technology and Software Services, India.
Printed in the UK.

ACKNOWLEDGEMENTS

I am indebted to a number of people in the support and capture of many of the images in this book. My wife, Avril, is my inspiration, my guide and my gear-carrying companion for many of my journeys and treks through the county and beyond. She is the steadfast deliverer of lens and camera changes as I see and try to capture the time-bound images in front of me, always looking for a perfect shot. My eldest daughter, Lorraine (also a photographer), has been a stand-in when those early-morning shots demand waking at 3 or 4 a.m. to travel to sites in the dark to be able to capture those unique impressions of sunrise.

Cheryl is my youngest and she keeps me in touch with the new technology and media developments so that I can successfully keep in touch with those who have followed my journey as Lightlog – with an aim to capture and replicate the light show that I see as I travel and note locations for future potential work.

Thanks are due to Amberley Publishing for noticing my work. Nick Grant in particular was instrumental in getting things in place. Also all the support I have received from friends, family and colleagues who have encouraged me to expand my reach with this book.

ABOUT THE PHOTOGRAPHER

Bryan Phillips is a proud Black Country man, growing up in the middle of the country among the steel-making industries the area is famed for. He has been the subject of a number of events showcasing his work, expressing his images through a variety of different media and formats.

'It's all about the light' is a significant phrase used by Bryan, relating to the natural light element that is so important in building his images for reproduction. This knowledge brings the realisation that each location has a series of potential results depending on the immediate light conditions and so a return to the same location builds a library of images that can look quite different. Being an 'early bird', sunrise is an important time for him and you will see the results of some of these in the following pages.

In his daily life, Bryan is a marketing and sales professional in the technology industry and this is where his association with Kent began. Bryan always has a camera at the ready. Therefore, travelling through and around the county (as well as the world), there are often opportunistic captures that await the ever-ready photographer. Of course there are those that were missed when time pressures or mode of transport meant that a halt was not possible, even if only for a moment.

Bryan has successfully presented images for the BBC, a US backpackers' guide and various projects around the country, but he still enjoys the buzz of a gallery show where visitors often remark on the detail found in the canvases and prints on display.

'Photography is my escape, my safe place, my creative release and I hope that you will be able to see some of that as you look through the images and notes in this book. I have been involved in photography from an early age, growing up with a Kodak Brownie bellows camera and developing my own images either in the loft or darkroom-converted bathroom. Modern equipment is much more versatile and allows high-quality images to be more frequently captured.'

The images in this book have been captured using a variety of cameras, lenses and attachments. Some of these are below:

Cameras: Nikon D850/Nikon D800/Nikon D810/Nikon D700/Nikon D300
Lenses: Nikkor AF-S 24–120mm/Nikkor AF-S 16–35mm/Nikkor AF-S 70–300mm/Nikkor 200–500mm
Accessories: Giottos MML3290B Monopod/Tiffen Filters

INTRODUCTION

Kent is such a diverse county, but full of captivating images from coast to country and beyond. It is known as the Garden of England and you will see images from this aspect, including both crops and locations that echo the essence of the county.

Magical and historic references abound, with ancient sites, defences and natural phenomenon giving a breadth of fascination among the wide number of influences around the area. In researching this book I came across a historic site older than Stonehenge in the north of the county. There are also undefeated castles, remnants of war, untouched natural beauty and ingenuity among its jewels. Roman influence is visible from the size and grandeur of Richborough Fort, one of the first Roman bases in England, to tantalising locations such as Reculver on the north Kent coast. Road tracks, ancient and modern, show their heritage with strong influences still in full view.

Moving into the core of Kent, nature and history combine to give the visitor a look back in time. Along the way, you may well trip over something unusual or even unique, ranging from windmills with sweeps rather than sails to pub games like Bat and Trap, an old English game still played in the county.

Finally, the vast 350-mile coast of Kent brings astonishing views, beauty and historic references. The white cliffs are synonymous with Dover and England but stretch far beyond the busy port, and have views across to our French neighbours. But I fear that I am keeping you from the true purpose of this book: to give an insight into the fascinating county of Kent.

RIVER AND COAST

Rocks in the bay, Herne Bay coast

Walking the coast, Samphire Hoe

Last light, Capel-le-Ferne cliffs

Tide remains, Dymchurch Beach

Kingsdown Beach

Echoes of the past, Dover Historic Cliff Trail

Martello tower, Folkestone

Shadows of history, Reculver Towers

Seaside view, Samphire Hoe

Wetland habitat, Pegwell Bay

Early manoeuvres, Port of Dover

White cliff coastline, Viking Bay

Oare Marshes

Discovered cove, Kingsdown

Morning welcome, Dover Harbour and seafront

Moorings, Faversham Creek

Night vision, Dover

Deal Pier

Edge of the map, White Cliffs of Dover

Sunrise over Regulbium's Roman fort

Royal Harbour, Ramsgate

Fisherman's rest, Deal Beach

Wildlife, Oare Marshes

TOWN AND COUNTRY

Olde worlde, The Old Weavers' House, Canterbury

Devil's Punchbowl, Wye

Brockhill Country Park

Stodmarsh National Nature Reserve

Casemate structures, Drop Redoubt Fort, Western Heights of Dover

High over the Wye Valley

On the whistle, Hythe

Butter Market, Canterbury

Nineteenth hole, Royal Cinque Ports Golf Club, Sandwich Bay

Miniature railway, Dungeness

Caesar's Camp, Folkestone

Great Cauldham Farm, Folkestone

Shine a light, The Butts, Sandwich

Bluebell woods, Ashford

Walmer Castle and Gardens

Wye Valley

Canterbury Cathedral

White Mill, Sandwich

Sandwich Town Cricket Club

Green pastures, Bodsham

Bleriot landing spot, Dover

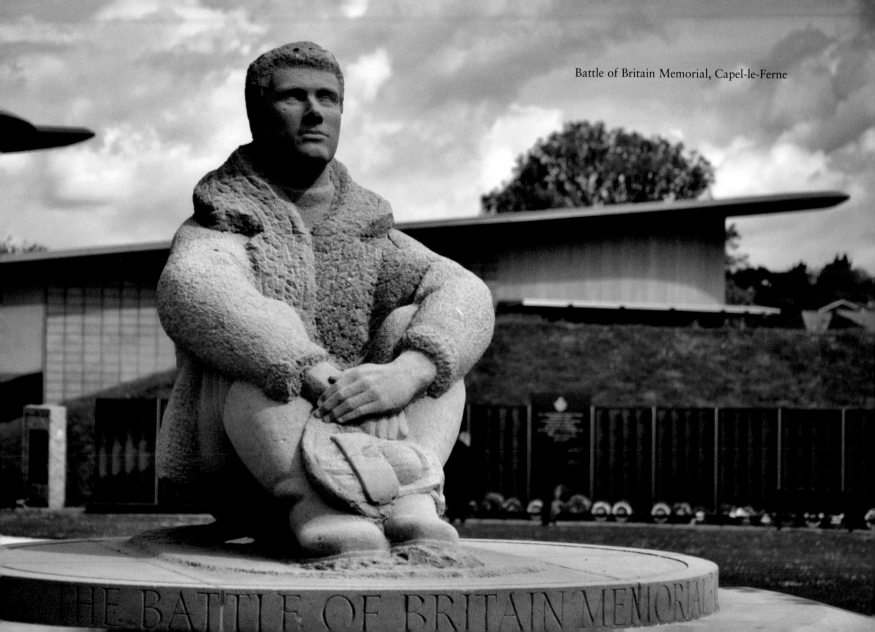

Battle of Britain Memorial, Capel-le-Ferne

Harvest time, Alkham Valley

Early mist, The Quay, Sandwich

Davison's Mill, Stelling Minnis

Ashford woodland

Orchard, Elmstone

Orchard, Preston

Power down, Port Richborough and Pegwell

Church on the marsh, Fairfield

The Salutation, Sandwich

Mill Wall, Sandwich

SECRET SPACES

Shakespeare Cliff, Aycliffe

St Thomas's Hospital, Moat Sole, Sandwich

Secret garden, Sandwich

Approach to Dover Castle

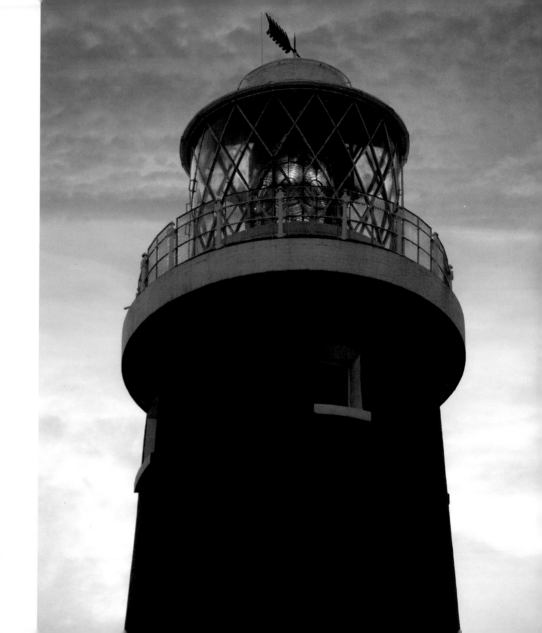

Dungeness Lighthouse

Walled garden, St Clement's

The clubhouse, Royal Cinque Ports Golf Club

Island home, Leeds Castle

Dry moat, Walmer Castle

The Warren, Folkestone

Sea stack, Joss Bay

Queen's Chapel window, Dover Castle keep

Coldrum Long Barrow, Trottiscliffe

A Spitfire and Hurricane over Lydd

Hidden cottage, Biddenden

Ancient steps, Richborough Roman Fort

Deal seafront

Chillenden Windmill

Market Square, Sandwich

Dubris Pharos (Roman lighthouse), Dover Castle

River Stour, Sandwich

HERE AND THERE

Red sky at night, Minnis Bay

Batten down the hatches, Dungeness

The Bulwark, Sandwich

Sky writing, Western Docks, Dover

Country Trail, Womenswold

Oast houses, Goudhurst

Sails in the sky, Chillenden Windmill

Up on the downs, North Downs, East Brabourne

Blean Woods, Canterbury

Out to sea, Folkestone

Mature brew, hop field, Goudhurst

Royal Harbour, Ramsgate

Dawn glory, Dover Harbour

The Quay, Sandwich

Blean Woods, Canterbury

Waiting game, Oare Marshes

Old Oast, Preston

Flight of the bumblebee, Walmer Castle Gardens

Wetlands, Stodmarsh

White cliffs, Dover

Langdon

Crop mechanics, Cauldham Farm, Capel-le-Ferne

Elmley Nature Reserve

West Pier Lighthouse, Ramsgate

Garden pride, Quex Park Gardens

Blean Nature Reserve

Snow leopard, Howletts Wild Animal Park, Bekesbourne

Brockhill Country Park, Sandling

Gathering the harvest, Waltham

The Swale

Over the edge, East Cliff, Dumpton Bay

Moored on the Swale

Autumn gold, Mote Park,
Maidstone

Country pathway, Hythe

Fisherman's Wharf, River Stour

Eurotunnel, Newington, Folkestone

Sunset over Elham